Rituals from the North

First Edition

ISBN: 9798851171307

D1522525

Produced by
The Fellowship of Northern Traditions

Edited and Formatted by
Jacob Toddson and Logan Osborne

Additional Editing by
Lauren Gamble and Aayla Kaisk

RITUALS FROM THE NORTH

Rituals from the North

Rituals from the North

Forward

By Jacob Toddson

The Fellowship of Northern Traditions is now a government recognized 501 c(3) non-profit with "church" status that seeks to re-create spiritual practices of the ancient world. But it has not always sounded so official; it all began in March of 2020, when nine individuals came together with the intention to hail the Norse Gods. They stood together around a fire and did their best to honor the beliefs of people who lived over a thousand years ago in a land thousands of miles away. Since that first event, before we were officially The Fellowship of Northern Traditions, we would hold many small private events around Kentucky and Ohio that oversaw rituals being performed for the various deities within the ancient Northern European world.

As the number of our gatherings and rituals grew, so did the number of individuals that would one day become official leaders within the community. Despite our growing leadership, we held true to the belief that our hierarchy is very simple. The Fellowship Leaders plan and host events, while also assisting in the administrative tasks required of an organization. Otherwise, ritual performance and taking lead in ceremonies have always been something we have left open for members of the community to assist with. This is one of the reasons we have decided to compile some of our rituals from the last few years into this book you are reading now.

This book has been written by the Fellowship Leaders and members of the community. This book was then formatted and edited primarily by myself and Logan Osborne. Please keep this in mind as you read each section, as the tone will most likely change depending on the author of that particular section. Our primary objective when publishing this book is to leave a legacy for generations to come, so that others will not need to learn from next-to-nothing like we have had to in this modern era. The mystery of the past is what attracts many of us to the old pagan paths, however the lack of literacy and written source material is one of the reasons we struggle to practice these beliefs today.

Please also keep in mind that we are writing many of these rituals from the perspective of group participation, but we have done our best to record these moments in a way that can be re-created as a solo practitioner. So do understand that not all of these rituals are "perfect" fits for the solo practitioner, but we hope they can still inspire you within your own personal practice.

With that, I would like to welcome you to read ahead and get started with whatever ritual or section you would like. However, first we will share a section on defining "ritual" and how we use it within this book. This section will be for those who wish to know more about our group interpretation and understanding of ritual practice.

Claire Beukinga, Netherlands 2022

On Ritual
By Mary Grace

The rituals that will be expanded upon in this book are of a spiritual nature, as opposed to mundane rituals such as making the bed. Performing ritual is a sacred act to honor the Gods, Ancestors, Folk or Spirits. Anyone can create and perform ritual ceremonies alone or in a group. Group ritual differs greatly from personal ritual in that it brings others in who have varying experience, but both share the purpose of honoring the subject of reverence. Group ritual involves multiple people with differing roles; the simplest of these roles are participant and ritual leader. Oftentimes there are also those who help create and manage the sacred space, play instruments, and offer invocations. At its simplest, group ritual is a team effort to honor the subject of reverence.

Ritual ceremony has been something humans have partaken in since before humans were humans.

Human history is ritual history.

From the east, west, north, and south - in all directions there were, and still are, oral stories that have been passed down from generation to generation. These oral histories are also forms of ritual ceremonies that honor ancient Gods and Goddesses, the Ancestors, those considered family, the Spirits of home and nature, as well as the cycles of life and death itself.

9

One example of what we might consider a "Folk" honoring ritual is burying the dead. It is well known that even the ancient people of the Stone Age and beyond would honor the dead with flowers and proper burials. Ritual is encoded within human nature.

When it comes to the past, there are certainly details that are either unclear or never to be recovered; many spoken traditions have collapsed, many people have assimilated into other cultures, and many wise elders were unable to pass their knowledge down. However, the old ways truly never left us. The old ways are still within us.

Entering altered states of consciousness and connecting with the land and higher powers is human nature. The knowledge of our Ancestors is at least partially accessible to us - in part due to the work of scholars, but also simply because we draw breath. There are many traditions around the world that we are unable to witness, and we can either lament in anguish endlessly over deceased traditions lost to time - or we can create our own. Connection did not leave us. We have the power to forge our own path forward, while still honoring the roots of our traditions.

Ceremonial structure

Establishing sacred space is important for any ceremony. Sacred space is dual purpose; it sets the space apart from other spaces for those in attendance and welcomes the subject of reverence. Similar to how a good host makes the home inviting to a guest, so too we make the space for our subjects of reverence. In the *Voluspa en Skama* of the <u>Prose Edda</u>, there is some historical evidence of building shrines for a deity:

"Ottar made me
An altar of stone,
And the stones of that temple
Glisten like glass,
Reddened with fresh blood
From sacrificed oxen-
Ottar believed faithfully
in the Goddesses (Freyja)."
~Voluspa en Skama 10
(Translation by Dr. Jackson Crawford)

These lines are spoken from the perspective of Freyja, who raises a dead witch in order to help Ottar, the man who built the shrine and offered it to the Goddess. This beautiful shrine and offering intended to honor the Goddess Freyja, and the Goddess in turn honored him by performing magic and seeking the answers he sought. This is a blessing, and the Gods and Goddesses do bless us and take notice when we honor them. The ritual space increases the likelihood of the subject of reverence looking upon our efforts favorably.

Commonly, this ritual space is created out of what is available. Stones are moved, candles are lit, incense is burned, and the area is hallowed by the ritual leaders for their purposes. Ritual space can be as simple as a campfire, personal altar, or even a special place in nature. Hallowing can be done with smoked herb bundles, incense, or sound, along with prayer to the

Gods, Goddesses, or Spirits to be honored in the space. Some feel most comfortable also crafting a circle or other metaphysical visible, or invisible, container for energy - clearing the previous energy, making way to invite our honored guests to receive offerings.

In preparing for ritual, participants and ritual leaders often get dressed in "ritual garb" or simply "garb." The ritual garb from person to person varies wildly. The garb, from an animistic point of view, is said to have a spirit of its own. These items can be staves and wands, skirts and shirts, shoes and headdresses, paint and furs. Ritual garb can play many roles for the person wearing it: protection, wisdom, divine communication, and other blessings as the wearer sees fit to enchant onto themselves. The act of putting on ritual garb helps many in preparing the mind for the coming ritual.

Ritual garb is not required to put on your ritual, or to attend one The Fellowship of Northern Traditions holds. We have had many people attend one of our events in only their "normal" clothes. We find that ritual garb is a natural process that will evolve and grow in time. Don't rush into it, feel it necessary, or buy into popular trends. Do what feels right to you, and what you feel honors the spirits.

Whether you are attending a ritual or hosting your own, it is a recommended practice to engage in grounding. Grounding is a practice that centers us into ourselves, bringing us into our bodies and into the present moment so that we might be able to receive the connection that we are after. To practice, think of grounding as a form of meditation, to feel the earth beneath your feet or tree within your hands and to grow your roots into the earth. Release the thoughts in your mind by placing yourself as the observer of them.

Breathe and prepare to receive.

Generally, our public rituals are loosely structured and allow lots of room for organic changes. Ritual ceremony begins with an introduction into who is being honored and why we would honor them. Introductions in public ritual contain additional background information on the importance of the deity, whereas personal ritual introductions are more specific to your relationship that you are either establishing or continuing. In the introduction phase we hope to call out to the subject of reverence to gain their attention for the ritual.

Following the introduction, the ritual moves into the offering stage. Offerings are gifts that are given to honor the ritual subject. These are given with great gratitude for the help, protection, blessings, time, and guidance that has been bestowed upon us by the honored guest. Offerings have a wide range of possibilities: crafted items, flowers, seeds, tobacco, stones, bones, incense, food, drink, etc. As a general rule of thumb, an offering must contain significance or meaning to the person giving the offering, something of value, but this does not necessarily mean expensive.

We advise that offerings be as natural as possible and would not harm the environment if left behind or burned in a fire. A popular tradition in Europe today is the tying of wishes to trees with ribbons. This is a beautiful tradition we would like to see practiced more. However, bio-degradable ribbons should be used so that they will not harm the environment. Materials such as cotton, hemp, or wool are examples of organic material. Nylon or polyester are examples of synthetic materials that could take hundreds of years to degrade.

Offerings are usually placed or poured onto a fire or onto the ground or in another designated place. They can also be consciously left in nature should they not harm the local environment. Within group rituals attendees are generally encouraged to share a few words about their offering or relationship with the subject of reverence.

Lastly, of course, is the conclusion. Ritual conclusions involve giving thanks to the subject of reverence and closing the ritual. The ritual leader will call out to the honored guests - Gods, Goddesses, Spirits, or Ancestors - one last time and reflect upon the ritual itself. Ritual closure is generally done with a final "hail!" call and response. This is typically the briefest component of ritual. Between the offering and conclusion stages we may involve drumming, dancing, or singing in order to honor the subject of reverence.

This format: introduction, offering, conclusion, has been humorously dubbed "the ritual sandwich." The ritual sandwich is not always adhered to within every ceremony, but it is a good general outline for ritual seeking to honor the Gods, Goddesses, Ancestors, or Spirits.

Notes on Ritual Etiquette

Ritual ceremony should usually be a serious affair. This does not mean we lose our senses of humor or the joy in our hearts, but that we are consciously making space for the honoring of the subject of reverence. A good group ritual leader will understand and persist through inevitable distractions such as unforeseen weather, children crying, or dogs barking. This will also be a discipline you will build through your own ritual practice. In life we can be hard pressed to find a quiet moment or space. To recenter yourself through distractions can be a form of practice that will deepen your relationship within spirituality.

Within group environments, cooperation and respect is paramount. Speaking or idle conversation is generally prohibited unless during offering; this includes the procession to the ritual location. The ritual leader should be unbothered except by persons helping with the ceremony as they are in their garb preparing for ritual. The ritual space should be minimally interfaced with after creation and prior to the ceremony. After the ritual, it is generally accepted to come towards the fire in contemplation or to mingle with the other participants.

Above all else, having respectful intentions towards the ritual leaders and participants helps to ensure that the most can be gained from the ritual.

The Format of this book

Now that we have covered some basics of ritual and ceremony, we will begin to present a selection of our various rituals performed throughout the years of our events. First will come seasonal rituals, as these are the most known celebrations of the ancient adherents to these beliefs.

Next will come rituals to honor the aforementioned Gods, Goddesses, Ancestors and Spirits. Then there will be a section titled 'Rites of Passage' that will include ceremonies both unique to the ancient world and also some that are practiced universally in cultures around the world.

Please keep in mind once again that these rituals were recorded by several individuals and formatted to be easy to read and digest. It is often hard to capture the full experience of a spiritual event in a few words, or even several hundred. We also wish to advise the reader that these rituals are going to be a mixture of historically referenced performances, along with some "neo-pagan" practices that have been helpful to pagans around the world. With that, let us begin in sharing our rituals and ceremonies with you!

SEASONAL RITUALS

Ritual to Freyr, Ohio 2021

Spring Freyr's Blót
By Caleb Baker and Logan Osborne

For the last few thousand years, spring has been the time of planting crops for cultures around the world. The structure of this ritual reflects the three stages of agriculture - the planting, tending, and harvesting of crops. It is suggested to give three offerings in accordance with these three elements of agriculture. The intention behind this ritual is to call to Freyr for blessings regarding a seed in your mind - something you wish to plant, nurture, and harvest in the year to come.

Naturally, many of us are no longer farmers in this modern age. However, this does not prevent us from reflecting upon these three stages of creation and the development of our work. We recommend using this ritual to place positive intentions in your creative hobbies or professional aspirations. While this ritual was performed publicly with several dozen people in attendance, it could be easily adapted for a personal practice.

With three small offerings you can sit in front of your altar, or somewhere within nature, and call out to Freyr and his many aspects. Once you feel you have connected, then you can share your three offerings while reflecting on the planting, the tending, and harvesting of your ideas. Or, perhaps you are actually planting crops - even better!

It is important to not rush through the three stages of the offerings, and use this time to reflect on what you wish to accomplish. To then follow through after the ritual and tend to your ideas, crops, or aspirations is another way to honor the aspects of Freyr and the growing season. If you are looking for inspiration on what to say for such a ritual, we will provide what was said at Ohio at a spring gathering in 2021. Feel free to adapt this invocation for your own needs.

Invocation

We have gathered here to honor the Vanir god Freyr. A man's man, a man who seeks to watch other people grow. The Horned God, the Stag God, and one of the Golden Twins. God of Agriculture and All That Grows, both people and plants alike. We are here tonight for Ostara, the beginning of a new cycle.

The Planting - it is time to plant the seed of what we want to grow, who we want to be, in the coming year. One must take considerations - if you have a good seed but plant it in the wrong place, a place without love, the seed will not grow, it will stagnate and die. Take the seed that you have in your mind for the coming year, plant it in a place of love, a place that is fertile and great, a place where it will become whatever you want it to be. But planting is not enough. You must tend to the seed as well.

Give the first offering

The Tending - Without proper care, no matter how well you plant your seed, it will fail to bring a bountiful harvest. It will wither and die. It needs to be cared for, it needs to be watered, it needs to be weeded, and allowed to grow free, without hindrance. That goes the same for people as it does for plants. Any idea that you wish to harvest in the coming cycle - it has to be tended to. So let the care for your seed be just like the whiskey to this fire, and be the fuel to a bountiful harvest.

Give the second offering.

The Harvest - Ingvi-Fryer, Shining Sun, and Rain-Clad Lord of the Vanir, God-King of Alfheim! God of the Harvest. Jera. The Returning of the Year. Tonight we have brought offerings for you. Harvest - many people think of it as the end, but in a way, it is also the beginning. Time to collect the strongest seeds, so that in the next year, the yield will be even stronger. Let us plant those seeds tonight, and recognize the turning of Jera. Freyr, be with us!

The third offering is given. After each offering, there is a communal "Hail Freyr!"

Hail Ingvi-Freyr! Thank you for our coming harvest this year, and may all the harvests to come be as bountiful as this one.

Ingvi-Frey, I offer you this platter of fruit. I hope that the wishes I heard from the folk tonight are not just dreams of thought, but dreams that they can enact. Seeds that they can tend to. I hope that I can watch them reap the harvest, and that we may celebrate together. Hail to you Ingvi!

Before we go off and reflect on tonight, and our plans to enact those thoughts, may we all give one more beastly howl that will give the God of the Fields and the Forest pride!

One more beastly howl that will give the God of the Fields and the Forest pride!

Final Thoughts

Freyr has very few stories that survive in written source material. However, according to early historians, Freyr was a great lord over humanity. He would see that his kingdoms had peace, prosperity, and fertility. Any ritual to him is better served if it calls to one, or more, of these aspects.

Spring Green Man Ritual
By Maya Hany

This ritual was performed in Scotland in April 2023. We were lucky to have a beautiful old oak grove as a place to honor the Green Man which was incredibly special due to his association with oak trees/leaves. Oak groves have historically been a place to gather together for learning, celebration, and ritual and we wanted to continue this tradition.

April is the time that the land starts to come to life again after winter has taken its toll. The oak grove was full of the first signs of spring, greeting us with an abundance of daffodils, wildflowers, and the sound of lambs bleating in the nearby fields.

The Green Man as a concept is something that transcends cultures, as evidence of his reverence has been found from the Middle-East to the northern reaches of Europe. While there are many renditions and modern fairy tales of the Green Man, the main attribute is the rebirth of nature every year after winter.

The idea behind this ritual was to aid in awakening the land, showing our respect, connection to nature, and acknowledgement of the change of the seasons as well as within ourselves. These are all elements that The Green Man represents. This was also an opportunity to celebrate coming together in a land that is incredibly special for so many of us.

Green Man Ritual, Scotland 2023

This ritual aimed to be full of joy in reflection of the start of the new season and the lighter times ahead of us.

The song that was written for this ritual aimed to take the listener on a journey through the darker months to Spring, as well as acknowledge that The Green Man survived the suppression of pagan beliefs and practices.

The Ritual

We gathered by a tree at the start of a small trail to the oak grove. Bells and "fairy sticks" (sticks with bells and ribbons attached to the top) were handed out. We then started our journey to the oak grove while skipping, dancing, waving our fairy sticks, and making joyful noise with our bells and voices.

Towards the start of the oak grove we made a small safe area to give offerings to The Green Man while the noise and fun atmosphere continued. We danced and laughed while offerings were being left.

We then gathered in the oak grove and everyone was encouraged to safely interact with the trees while the following song was performed:

"As the icy tendrils grip the ground
And the nights are cold and long
Some days it takes all our strength to stand
And remember our joy and song

- Oh this way the Green Man comes

The ground is so hard it feels like stone
The berries wither on the bramble
The forests are barren, their leaves far blown
The creatures tonight must scramble

- Oh this way the Green Man comes

As the first green shoots are sprouting
And the mornings are lighter and free
We feel the rebirth of all around
The land, ourselves, and thee

- Oh this way the Green Man comes

The fragrant scent of the elder
The comforting spring of the moss
Life is returning to everything
And we put aside things we've lost

- Oh this way the Green Man comes

He watched over those before us
Now his face is etched in stone
Peering through pews and towers
Wild spirits are never alone

- Oh this way the Green Man comes

When you feel the calming sense of home
As you walk through the birch and oak
Give thanks to him as you do roam
For the trees, the streams, the folk

The line "Oh this way The Green Man comes" was sung in unison and this was discussed before the ritual began. We then spent some time in the oak grove appreciating the nature around us before heading back along the short trail to tie ribbons on the tree where we initially gathered. Tying ribbons to trees is a custom linked to the nature spirits, fertility, and appeasing the fae.

This ritual can of course be performed solo, and remembering this song to sing among the forest and meadows could be a wonderful way to enchant the spirits of nature, on top of being a way to honor the idea of The Green Man.

Sif Blót, Ohio 2023

Summer Sif Blót

By Mary Grace and Logan Osborne

This blót was performed at the Fellowship of Northern Traditions Pennsylvania Midsummer Gathering in August of 2022. The gathering took place in forests and fields under the hottest days of the summer and under a full moon. This was a very appropriate time to honor the often overlooked goddess Sif. Full moons towards the end of summer were a common time in the past for communities to gather and collectively perform the first harvest. Crops were ripening and the full moon provided light for reaping well into the night. In the spirit of this season, a blót to Sif was held to honor the history of our farming ancestors and their prayers to the goddess of the fields.

A special ritual fire pit and altar was built in preparation for this ritual. The altar included a votive candle depicting Sif, shafts of wheat, farming tools, bread, and beer. The ritual leaders offered bread, beer, and an antique sickle to the goddess. Folk in attendance gave a variety of offerings, most commonly bread and beer to commemorate the gifts of the fields. Drums were played as the folk gave their offerings. The fellowship leaders each carried scythes, which were placed in the shape of Jera, the harvest rune, around the fire pit while offerings were given.

This ritual can easily be adapted to be performed alone. Building an altar or other sacred space devoted to Sif as the ritual leaders did in this case can be a great opportunity to reflect on the importance of the gifts of Sif as the goddess of the fields. We will provide you with a rough transcription of what we said below!

Invocation

We have gathered under sweltering sun and full summer moon. For thousands of years, our ancestors gathered under the same sun, and the same moon. They gathered, toiled, sweat, and laughed long into the night. They worshiped and gave thanks to the goddess of the fields - Sif.

Sif, Golden-Haired Goddess of grain, we thank you for your gifts. Our ancestors' bone and flesh were borne of your gifts. Wheat, oats, barley, rye, hay, flax, and straw. We use your gifts to make bread, beer, linen, clothing, and food for our livestock. So great are your gifts Sif that surely, without you we would perish.

Our ancestors knew this well. In their tales of the end times, of Ragnarok, the event that finally drives men mad and makes them spill their brother's blood is the Fimbulwinter. The long winter in which the ground is frozen solid and the fields bear no fruit. Our ancestors feared your absence, and they praised your presence. Sif, great goddess, we thank you.

Wife of Thor, Mother of Ullr, Scythe Charmer, Trickster Shorn, Gold Adorned, Life Abundant, She Who Feeds Us.

Hail Sif!

Folk, if you have offerings for Sif, come forth and give to the fire!

(For solo practitioners, this is a moment to tell Sif that you have brought her offerings)

All present come forth and give offerings to the ritual fire.

Thank you for your offerings to the seldom-remembered goddess Sif. As we continue to gather here, remember that the ancestors live through you. We gather as they once did - to hail the gods.

Hail the ancestors!

Hail the folk!

Hail Sif!

Final notes

Even in modern times, when most of the population is removed from the toil of farm labor, we are surrounded by Sif's bounty on a daily basis. From the cotton and linen shirts we wear to the rolls and beer we enjoy at dinners with friends and family— Sif's gifts are many. Giving these gifts back to the goddess allows one to bask in gratitude for the hard work of our fellow human beings and the graciousness of the goddess who feeds and clothes us. When giving to her, consider what sorts of treasures and abilities you wish to tend to and harvest to provide for yourself and share with the ones you love. Picture your offering to the golden-haired goddess of grain as planting a seed that, if carefully tended to, will someday ripen into these gifts - just as our ancestors once viewed their community's golden fields of grain.

Hail Sif!

Summer Maypole Ritual

By Lauren Gamble

The Maypole is one of the few pagan traditions that has survived throughout the conversion era and is still practiced frequently today. In Sweden for instance, Midsummer is often considered the most important celebration of the year. Maypoles have existed in many Germanic and Scandinavian countries; Maypole dances also come in just as many variations across Europe. Beltane is also a common holiday where Maypoles are featured, celebrated on May 1st.

There are a few variations of the "Beltane" story, and its origins are widely debated. Common stories can include the May Queen and the Green Man, the Oak King and the Holly King, or with the ancient Celtic God Belenus. Regardless of origin or motif, the main focus of Beltane is on the changing of the seasons, and the celebrations of the sun's return.

Some countries utilize another Beltane tradition of a large bonfire, but Maypoles are still used most notably by Sweden and Bavaria across their summer celebrations.

Maypoles themselves are a large but simple pole decorated by greenery and flowers, with a circle or two to tie long ribbons around to hang. These ribbons are typically left long enough for participants to pick up the ends and hold them through the Maypole dance, twisting and weaving the ribbons into a unique pattern.

Maypole Ritual, North Carolina 2022

During the dance as each ribbon runs out of room to weave that participant steps back, and whoever is the last standing weaver is crowned the May Queen. Some choose to leave the ribbons shorter and do choreographed dancing in a circle about the pole instead. The commonality of Maypole celebrations is in the utilization of the pole itself, things that grow, and merry-making with the community.

Ritual

Maypole rituals are best conducted in a group setting, but there are simpler ways to honor the tradition alone as well. Simply craft a miniature version of the Maypole to decorate and use as a focal point for an altar or private ritual, or incorporate ribbon and flowers into your solo celebration. You could even have a full size Maypole if you're able, and leave offerings at the base while you dance around it and call to the Gods and Spirits. Weave yourself a flower crown and spend time outside enjoying the sun's warmth.

If you have a group to celebrate with, circling around the Maypole with or without ribbons is a light-hearted and simple way to honor the ancient traditions. You may play music or have a drummer to keep the pace and encourage dancing. Summer is a season of joy and fun, so these kinds of community building activities come naturally to the spirit. Take the time to enjoy the beautiful weather outside, partake in crafting together, and above all cherish the sacred time with your community.

Små Grodorna (Little Frogs)
By Jacob Toddson

In Sweden one of the most popular dances/songs to perform during Midsummer is the "Little Frogs" dance. This dance is meant to be a fun and energetic start to any Midsummer celebration; while it's not necessarily spiritual in nature, it still calls to the spirit of the holiday. The dance is also conducted around a Maypole traditionally.

You can find many versions of "Små Grodorna" to listen to, but here is the Swedish and English Versions:

[Swedish]

*"Små grodorna, små grodorna är lustiga att se.
Små grodorna, små grodorna är lustiga att se.
Ej öron, ej öron, ej svansar hava de.
Ej öron, ej öron, ej svansar hava de.
Kou ack ack ack, kou ack ack ack,
kou ack ack ack ack kaa.*

[English]

*"The little frogs, the little frogs are funny to observe.
The little frogs, the little frogs are funny to observe.
No ears, no ears, no tails do they possess.
No ears, no ears, no tails do they possess.*

*Kou ack ack ack, kou ack ack ack,
kou ack ack ack ack kaa."*

Små Grodorna Dance, Ohio 2023

Autumn Blót to the Gods of Death

By Logan Osborne

This ritual was designed to be performed at the Kentucky Fall Gathering in 2022, near the Gaelic holiday of Samhain. This time of year, midway between the fall equinox and winter solstice, was viewed as a time when the veil between the worlds of the living and the dead was thinnest. With this in mind, the idea was formed for a ritual devoted to the gods associated with death. The order to which the gods are invoked and offered to is meant to reflect the mythological motif of a journey into the underworld. Six fires were lit for the purpose of offerings, with the participants walking a candlelit path between the fires to further symbolize a journey to the land of the dead. Upon completion of the offerings to the gods, a letter is offered by each participant to an ancestor to whom they wish to send a message.

Nerthus, the Germanic goddess often attributed as the mysterious "sister-wife" of the Norse god Njord, is first invoked. She is a veiled goddess of a dichotomous nature - when her oxcart moved throughout the lands, violence was frowned upon, but at the end of her procession, humans were sacrificed in her name. As a veiled goddess of life and death, she is invoked to "lift the veil" for the ritual participants, allowing access to the realm of the dead.

Next invoked are Freyja and Odin, both known in the myths to make journeys to the realm of the dead to seek counsel of beings residing there. Odin famously journeys to the underworld in the *Völuspá* to resurrect and seek the divinations of a dead völva, or seeress, while Freyja makes a similar journey in the *Völuspá hin skamma*. Both are also associated with collecting the souls of those who die in battle, Odin bringing them to his hall Valhǫll, and Freyja to the meadow Fólkvangr.

Following the invocations to the gods who journey to the land of the dead, invocations are made to two gods who reside there - Nanna and Baldur. These married deities arrived in Hel following the tragic death of Baldur, and reside there until Ragnarok. Nanna, known for joining Baldur on his funeral pyre from grief, is passionately invoked to honor her and the emotions of grief, heralding the arrival of the ritual participants to the realm of the dead. Baldur is invoked in a more joyous manner, signifying the recognition that those separated by death will once more meet.

The last invocation is made to Hel, ruler of the realm of the dead. Hel is honored as the gentle but fierce guardian of the ancestors, and the offerings given to her are both to honor her and to ask that the messages from the folk be given swift passage to the ancestors.

The veil is lifted, the journey is undertaken, the dead gods honored, and finally, the Queen of the Dead, Hel, is revered. Finally, the ritual participants give letters they have written to an ancestor or beloved dead to the fire. They have completed the mythological journey to the

Gods of Death Ritual, Kentucky 2022

underworld, and are rewarded with an opportunity to express their grief and love, and perhaps receive wisdom from their honored dead. Of course, ancestor worship can be performed at any time of the year, and with less preparation. However, a ritual of this magnitude is meant to honor the gods, seeking their favor at the time when the realm of the dead is most accessible, so as to create a powerful spiritual space in which communication with the dead is, hopefully, most successful.

To perform this ritual solo, we recommend having an altar space (inside or out) where you can light six fires to these six Gods of death. At the lighting of each candle you can leave a small offering and reflect on each deity for a time before moving on. This ritual was long to perform in person for over thirty people, and it should be a longer ritual that we recommend taking your time with, possibly even setting aside an hour or two in order to fully absorb the sacredness of the fall season. Below will be a transcript of what was said during the ritual for each deity if you are looking for inspiration.

Nerthus

In ancient days a veiled goddess rode by oxcart through hills and valleys, village and forest. Men lay down their weapons of war upon word that her procession moved through the land. All those who saw her face drowned. Tonight we drown our spirits in the deep waters of the realms of death. We seek the mysteries of birth and decay. And so first I invoke and honor the Veiled Matron of the Vanir, the Bog Queen, Goddess of the Great

Churning. From peat and sludge and ash springs new life. From bones our bones are born. This is the dominion of Nerthus, the mysterious goddess of the cycle of life and death. Nerthus, lift the veil and cast your drowning gaze upon us. We honor you, and ask that you allow us passage and return to the cairns of our ancestors.

Nerthus, I give you this offering that your cart may ride and the veil be lifted tonight.

Hail Nerthus!

Come to the bonefire and give to Nerthus!

Freyja

Now we journey to the misty fields of the fallen. But our feet are far from first to tread these roads. We walk in the footprints of gods who made the long trek to the gates of Helheim. The Falcon Queen, Freyja, Seidmaster, the Amber Weeper once walked this road to cast her fiery spells in a magic duel with a dead giantess. Remember, folk, that Freyja takes first pick of the slain. Freyja, teach us as you taught the Allfather!

Guide our steps to the land of the dead! May we move with silent falcon flight to the gravemounds. Vanadis! Fill our hearts with love, swell our spirits with magic, ignite our eyes ablaze with beauty, and light our paths with gleaming tears.

Freyja, I give you this offering that you aid us with death charms tonight.

Hail Freyja!

Come to the bone-fire and give to Freyja!

Odin

Can you hear the grave-birds croaking? Can you hear the howl of the cairn-dogs? The Allfather beckons.

For the Allfather too is wise in the mysteries of death. Like Freyja, he felt the stones of the road to Hel beneath the footfalls of his steed. He bade the volva's bones rise from their tomb. He gathers the slain Einherjar in Valhol. He whispered charms and soaked herbs in the severed head of his wise uncle Mimir, that he may always seek counsel of the honored dead. He keeps near his throne the divine scavengers Hugin, Munin, Geri, and Freki. He sacrificed himself on Yggdrasil, the World Tree. Odin! God of the Gallows, Hrafnaguð, Draugadróttinn, Farmr Galga, Lord of Asgard! Cast your fiery eye upon us as we seek words with the dead! May your ravens soar in the winds of Hel tonight!

Odin, I give you this offering that on this night we may slip through realms as you do.

Hail Odin!

Come to the bonefire and give to Odin!

Nanna

Folk, listen. Do you hear the silence? The grave-birds have ceased their croaking. Now, they only weep. They know she walks among us. Close your eyes. Do you see the darkness? Do you see the flickering light on the horizon? A ship burns. Breathe deep. Do you smell it? Perfumed soot fills the air. The charred robes of the Priestess of the Pyre float on mournful winds. Nanna beckons. Lady of Lamentation, Goddess of Grief, I beg you, take our broken and bruised hearts into your gentle embrace. Songs are sung of the glory of death, but the infinite history of all that lives and dies is soaked to the bone in tears. Tears borne of longing for lost peace. Mothers and fathers flickering from this realm before the tearful eyes of their children. Unborn babes and cherished lovers taken too soon. Nanna, wife of Baldur, knows your pain. When all wept, she leaped. She made a friend of fire when love departed. Nanna, wife of Baldur, we know your pain. We have all lost. We honor you, Nanna, Princess Among the Dead.

Nanna, I give you this offering that you may soothe us and those we've lost as we long for one another on this night.

Hail Nanna!

Come to the bone-fire and give to Nanna!

Baldur

I have spoken of the tears of the Grief Goddess, but know that in another time, another place, she weeps no longer. In the kingdom of the dead, she basks in lover's light once again. The Shining Son of Asgard, The Dead Prince, The Summer Son, Baldur, radiates in eternal glory in golden halls among our ancestors. Every tree and stone, every eagle, stag, and serpent wept and mourned the Spear-Gored Son of the High One and the Beloved. But like the summer, like the sunrise, like his own death, like our deaths, his return to the land of the gods is inevitable.

Baldur, I give you this offering that you may remind us that no matter the darkness, a new day always shines. That though death may be inevitable, so too is reunion.

Hail Baldur!

Come to the bone-fire and give to Baldur!

Hel

Now we arrive, as all things must, at the end. The great hall Eljudnir looms. We sit at her table, a dish called hunger and a knife named famine before us. Queen of the Dead, Cairn Mother, Great Goddess of the Grave, Hel, we come before you tonight as all children of Jord eventually must. We thank you for your tenderness as well as your fierceness as you watch over our beloved dead. We thank you for the lessons you teach us, that

45

darkness and light coexist, that the hail that rips the leaf so too waters the field. Bone Mother, bless us by parting your gleaming bale Blikjandobol before us believers on this night. We have walked the frigid road to your kingdom that we may praise you, that we may speak with our lost loves. Someday yet, each of us will walk this road again. Until that day, Mighty Hel, know that you are honored here amongst the living.

Hel, I give you this offering - from the world of the living to the Queen of the Dead - that the mead-halls and bonfires of Midgard and Helheim may unite tonight!

Hail Hel!

Come to the bonefire and give to Hel!

Folk, we have walked the road to Helheim. The veil is parted. Come forth and give your messages to your beloved dead to the bonefire.

(It is at this time you can give any additional offerings and spend time in their presence).

Hail to those on the other side!

Final Thoughts

This was a complex ritual to prepare for, with seven different fires along a path in the forest, and many invocations that had to be memorized by the ritual leader. I think the folk participating in the ritual were able to have a powerful ritual experience, but as the leader organizing the ritual, all the moving pieces were a little stressful.

Post Sunna Night Naps, Ohio 2022

Winter Sunna's Night Ritual

By Jacob Toddson

A Sunna night is a night long dedication to the Norse Goddess of the Sun, Sunna. It involves staying up and sacrificing your sleep as an offering. This ritual can also be dedicated to Heimdallr who must watch over Asgard, and look for signs of Ragnarok. We often forget that offerings do not always need to be physical objects, but can also be acts or deeds.

It is recommended that this ritual be performed during the longest night of the year (for the Northern Hemisphere this is usually December 21st) as this also can be used as a ritual to welcome the return of Sunna/ the Sun in spring. This ritual can be done alone, but is even more fun with friends, as it can be quite the challenge to keep each other awake to see the morning sun rise. This also makes the ritual something that can be done with non-pagan friends and family members, as it can be a fun challenge alongside a religious dedication.

This ritual does not have any basis in history, however we do know the ancient norse did track time via a lunar calendar, and only observed two seasons, summer and winter. This meant that Yule was one of the most important religious events for the peoples of the old north. Darkness and cold meant something different to these people as well; darkness limited activities outside and required people to spend more time inside with their friends and family. In the Scandinavian countries this could mean up to 20+ hours inside every day!

This ritual is meant to replicate that in some way, so while it is dedicated to Sunna, and possibly Heimdallr, it can also be a way to "live as the ancestors" for a night. It is also recommended to focus on activities such as board games, sports, or dance to keep each other awake and pass the time.

Unlike the previous sections this will not be a transcript of what was said during one of the performances of this ritual over the years, but a guide on how to perform it based on our experiences over the years.

Performance

To start the ritual, wait till sunset and gather those observing with you, facing towards the setting sun. Speak aloud to Sunna your intentions, and offer up your sleep to her; also declare that you will see the morning sun rise before going to sleep. It is at this time that you can offer any additional items as offering to either Sunna, or Heimdallr if you are invoking him as well.

After this you are free to go about the night, and do your best to stay awake! It is important to remember that this ritual is supposed to be a fun way to stretch your limits, and that it is perfectly okay to give into sleep. This is also why it can be fun to do with others because whoever stays awake will have bragging rights! In our experience with this ritual less than 50% of people that start the ritual, will finish it in the morning. So don't be too hard on yourself if you do not make it! Simply try again some other time.

For solo practitioners I recommend using this time to work on hobbies, crafts, or studies pertaining to pagan subjects. Perhaps you use this time to carve runes, make jewelry, draw, paint, or any other past-time you have not been able to practice in the last cycle. Even if you do not have any fellow pagans to do this with, it can be a great ritual to do with friends or family. Everyone likes a challenge, and then it can be even easier to stay awake as you all push through together!

Final Thoughts

Sunna Nights have been a staple of every Yule in the Fellowship of Northern Traditions, and it is our hope that it is a tradition that lives on in future generations. And maybe it can become a tradition in your homes and hearths as well. Happy Yule!

Disir Blót, Ohio 2022

Winter Disir Blót

By Aayla Kaisk

We all know of Frigg, the High One, the All-Mother, and recall how she wept and wailed at the death of her beloved Baldur. Focus your mind and hearts now on Frigg, the Cloud Weaver, Wise One, The Knower of Fates, and all the secrets she holds. Recall the Lokasenna and Freyja's warning to Loki:

"Frigg knows all fates, though she does not speak them." (v.29)

She is the only other being able to sit Hlidskjaf, Odin's High Seat, and peer upon all the worlds. She is of the Nornir, and the handmaidens are simply aspects of her being.

We all hail in frith, but do we know that the very meaning of frith hails from Her? The root is priya, the Proto-Indo-European root of Frigg. (Gundarson, Kveldoy) Spanning back to 4500-2500 BC we have known of her worship, so let us worship her again.

Disir Blóts are one of the oldest documented rituals in Scandinavia, going all the way back to the times of Uppsala in Sweden, at least in the later Viking age. The Disir are the female ancestors and spirits that guide and protect us. This ritual was performed in the middle of winter in February, during a time of returning light, and the coming spring. Disir Blóts are still performed in

Uppsala today by the modern Asatru Organization there.

The ritual I will share with you here is based off of the rendition put on during the Ohio Yule celebration (Yule is also a common time to have a "mother's night" ritual). It can of course be done by a solo practitioner who will take up each of the parts, and be in charge of memorizing the lines and small song, along with the giving offerings.

Ritual

You will need at least two candles, one for Frigg, and the other for your female ancestors. For our public ritual we had each participant have their own candle, lit by a main candle.

Begin with a steady drum beat; space is made sacred with the smoke of juniper, cedar, and rose.

"We come together tonight to honor Frigg, our All-Mother, Our Wise One, and her connection to the Fate-Weavers. We call out tonight to our Disir, honoring their memories, known and lost. As we light our candles, let the light shine down the lines of the women in our families, known and unknown, showing ourselves the paths to their wisdom. I call out to the women in my line (list names of your known female ancestors). Let me feel your strength and wisdom at my back, in my bones, and flowing through my blood. To pass on to our daughters, to our future mothers. Take your lights, calling on your lines, speak their names to float into the sky, calling yours to you."

Light a center candle for Frigg, then light your ancestral candle(s) with that flame. It is at this time you can give additional offerings as well.

Continue drum rhythm, and then begin to sing/chant this line until you feel you have either connected enough, or honored Frigg to an appropriate extent (I recommend at least nine times):

"Pull us Frigg into your distaff; twist us in your wheel;
Wise Frigg weave us into your web of wyrd;
Aesir Queen
Cloud Weaver, Sky Mother
Frigg, Frigg, Frigg."

It is at this point that we will begin to close the ritual space and thank Frigg, and the Disir for their sacrifice to us. You may use my closing as inspiration for your own:

"We call out to you Frigg, May we weave favorable futures, honor our disir, and raise the next generation to do the same. May the fires in our homes burn bright, our doors open to those of honorable intent, and our eyes be wise to protect our hearth and home. These offerings we give to you so that through the coming darkness we may be blessed with your wisdom and light."

Hail Frigg!

Hail the Disir!

GODS AND SPIRITS

Pre-Ritual, Kentucky 2022

The Gods

By Jacob Toddson

There is so much that can be said about the Gods of pagan beliefs; for the sake of this work and the rituals within it, I will do my best to summarize their general role in ritual practices.

As described by the Fellowship of Northern Traditions, we seek to venerate the Gods of Northern European beliefs— particularly the Norse Gods of Scandinavia. We also believe that the Gods of Celtic, Slavic, Germanic, and even Baltic and Finnish beliefs are so closely related that we can learn much from invoking them within ritual practices. This is not something shared by all pagan or heathen circles; many will only choose to worship the Aesir and Vanir deities exclusively. Others may choose to perform rituals for a wide variety of Norse beings including the Jotunn (Giants). As you have also seen in this work we have had rituals to beings such as "The Green Man" who is widely venerated in Europe and beyond.

Ultimately we seek to provide environments where anyone is allowed to explore their individual practice through the lens of Norse Cosmology. Meaning that all realms exist on the World Tree Yggdrasil, which can also be seen as the Spirit Realm of global shamanic traditions. It is on the branches of this world tree that the homes of the Gods exist, and where we too reach out to them from our home here in Midgard.

Often within rituals we seek to create spaces where these Gods can be called to spend time with us, hear our words, and receive our gifts. It is through this giving of gifts, and sharing our words, that we receive the guidance of the Gods. We will explore an "Open Blót" in the following section that will share with you how to connect to a specific deity of your choosing.

Otherwise, we will share with you several specific rituals that focus on one particular deity that we have developed rituals for. In the case of our "Vanir" and "Goddess" Blóts, we create rituals to target a group of deities whom we then invoke the names of during the course of the ritual.

Our aim with this section is to inspire you with our traditions and interpretations of source material, so that you can continue to develop your own practice. Feel free to use and adapt each of these rituals for your own use!

Open Blót
By Kat Jameson

Open Blóts have been in the community since our first few events, and have been common practice for many of our gatherings as they spread around the world. What this ritual allows people to do is to give to whatever deity they wish within the confines of the sacred space. This also allows people to share some about their personal experiences, if they wish, as they give an offering.

This type of ritual will also serve as a good basis for beginning practice on giving to a deity, or any spiritual presence, you are feeling like reaching out to. This ritual is highly customizable in both a group and private practice, as your items and environment can all play a part in how this ceremony takes place. It also pairs well with a meditation or trance before or afterwards. You can also incorporate items like drums, bells, or singing bowls. (This is my personal method of centering the mind beforehand.)

Once the space is set up as you would like, you can begin by cleansing the area as part of the ritual (counter-clockwise to remove, clockwise to imbue). To begin any ritual you must first call to the deities or beings that you are hoping to connect with. In a group environment, we would call to the general "gods" , "spirits", and "ancestors" who assist us in our spiritual journeys.

Once you have called out to the gods (or your singular specific being) you can proceed to give your offering.

Open Blót, Scotland 2023

After the offering is given, you can sit with the presence within your sacred space for as long as you'd wish. Asking them questions, sharing stories, or just meditating.

Once you have connected and taken your time, it is always important to thank the presence you have given to for their time as well. Then allow them to leave your space, and you can begin closing the ritual in the reverse of how you started it. This will of course change based on how you individually set up your own sacred space and ritual.

Safety and Protection

Fortunately, there are many precautions we are able to take when invoking spirits, gods, or other energies to avoid unintended side-effects that can cause harm. Not only do we have human spirits wandering among us pretty much everywhere we go, there are also entities who thrive and feed off of the unaware and unprotected. When you cast a circle or prepare a sacred space you are essentially sending out a beacon to the other realms. It's best to be cautious and better to be safe than sorry. There are simple steps you can take to avoid unwanted or negative entities from interfering with your ritual. The space should be cleansed and protected from spirits that would potentially interfere, harm, or leech off of the energy. Here's some basic information to guide you in your own path.

When first setting up the area where you plan to gather around for ritual there are a couple different ways to proceed. One option is casting a circle physically in the dirt, with candles (tea lights are perfect, light them with the intention of creating a barrier against the negative or unwanted spirits), or with smoke (incense or bundles).

In traditional heathen circles, the god Thor will be invoked with what is called a "hammer-rite," where a physical hammer is used to invoke a protective space and serve as an "anchor point" for the ritual itself. This can be adapted by yourself to include any deity you find to have protective qualities.

Final Thoughts

Open Blóts are as the name implies... open! They are highly customizable to your personal needs and desires within a ritual practice. They can be historical, or invoke modern practices that you find helpful within your own personal spiritual journey. So don't forget to have fun and allow your personal creativity to flow!

Odin Ritual, California 2022

Ritual to Odin

By Jacob Toddson

When looking at the stories within the *Poetic Edda,* there is a theme within the Odin stories of wisdom and memorization. When Odin went to face Vafþrúðnir, the wise jotunn, he sought to best him with wisdom and wits. We see this again in the poem *Grimnismal* when Odin shares yet more wisdom with Agnarr, a young boy who served Odin mead while he was imprisoned. Further still we see this in the poem *Havamal,* which is a series of lessons given to humanity from the mouth of Odin himself. What these stories paint for us comes to light once it is remembered that these stories were not always committed to writing, and had been passed down orally by skalds, priests, and jarls for hundreds and possibly thousands of years.

This too survives in the *Kalevala* of Finnish myth, which shows the immense amount of poetry that was once memorized by spiritual leaders, shamans, and kings. Lastly, I will add that the Druids of the Celtic world were also said to have committed everything to memory, and saw writing things down as a weakness of the mind. All of this leads us back to Odin, in that I believe one of the best ways to honor and connect with him, is to use your memory.

I have done this before in a ritual that pays homage to the knowledge shared in the *Havamal,* specifically in the section of wisdom given to a person named Lodfafnir. It is a series of wisdom and sorcery that is shared in a poetic style that was once memorized by skalds. The offering and ceremony of this ritual is the memorization and speaking of these verses.

Keep in mind that this can be done with dozens of written source materials, for example: the runes, the Eddas, the sagas, and phrases in old norse or other ancient languages. To me, the possibilities are nearly endless for things to remember and dedicate to the Hooded-One (Grimnir) himself! This, in my mind, is a perfect challenge for a solo practitioner because it will both sharpen your mind and grow a deeper connection with Odin through its practice and performance. It can also be a fun party trick to be able to recite old norse stories from memory!

What I will leave you with are the lines from the *Havamal* that I memorized for my Lodfafnir ritual; keep in mind that I have modernized them in English to make them more palatable. You can edit them further to fit your needs, just as every skald of the past would have done as well.

Lodfafnir's Wisdom

"Never rise in darkness, unless to spy on your enemies.

Never sleep in the arms of sorcery, you will wake frozen in fear.

Never seduce another's lover with whispers in their ears.

Rituals from the North

Always prepare to travel by the land or sea.

Never will your deeds profit from evil beings.

Always visit friends, or suffer from paths covered in weeds.

Learn healing charms while you live, they may save your life.

Loneliness will eat your heart, if your hearth is empty.

Never speak with a fool who will not see reason.

Keep goodness in your heart, and be regarded with praise.

Never fight a battle with a lesser man.

Build your own fires, and learn to live for yourself.

Never give your enemies peace while they sleep.

Never should you cherish bad news, always celebrate good news.

Never look up in a fight, or be cursed by your enemies.

Keep promises to your lovers to win their heart.

Beware the lies of others, and the strength of drink.

Never mock, nor laugh at a wanderer, for it may be Odin in disguise!

Do not become trapped in your.

Wise words often come from the mouths of grey beards.

Never spit on the hospitality of others.

When you drink beer choose the might of the earth!

The might of the earth will keep your head clear!

Fire will cure your sickness.

Oak will cure your bowel.

Wheat will ward off magic.

An Elder tree against Family.

Maggots against Venom.

Runes against evil.

Ground against water.

Swear beneath the moon!"

Final Thoughts

This ritual can be adapted in many different ways. For example I inserted the phrase: "At Odin's hall we heard them so!" between each line to break up the chant, and give myself time to remember the next line. Additionally you can add offerings, meditations, drums, music, or really any other ritual element to spice up your own version! Keep in mind that memorization takes time and practice, so don't think this is something you need to get right 100% the first go around. Don't be afraid to do this several times over the course of months or even a year.

Vanir Blót, Kentucky 2020

Vanir Blót

By Logan Osborne

This ritual was performed at the very first Yule gathering for the community that would become the Fellowship of Northern Traditions. It was our biggest gathering up to that point, with over fifty attendees. Like the other gatherings from that first year, many of the folk present grew to become long-lasting and honored members of the community.

The ritual was performed on the banks of a lake in mid-December. It ended with an impromptu group plunge into those cold waters, followed by a brisk hike back to the property's hot tub. The group plunge was unplanned, and a great example of how sometimes improvisation during rituals can lead to treasured memories.

Before the ritual, the ritual leaders - Logan, Zak, and Parker, built a large altar to each of the four Vanir deities being honored. After each offering, the group let out a communal "Hail!" for the god being offered to, which echoed magically against the distant shore of the lake. A bald eagle flew over the congregation mid-ritual. This was certainly one of those rituals that goes down as a magical memory for everyone involved.

The reason we wanted to have a ritual to the Vanir is because they are an often forgotten component of modern paganism, and have also been scarcely written of in historical sources as well. We know that they were a separate tribe of Gods consisting of at least Freyr, Freyja, Njord, and (possibly) Nerthus. Outside of their realm being Vanaheim and their connection to the natural world, little is known about what separated them from the Aesir Gods. Of course there are many theories around the Vanir and their origins, however when it comes to ritual we do not look to create or prove theories, but create experiences and new stories around these subjects.

As with previous sections, I will provide you with information on what we did for the group ritual, but I also believe it would be easy to recreate in a solo ritual with yourself in nature or at your altar. While at your altar you can take a moment to reflect on the four known Vanir, and give small offerings to each with moments of reflection in between. One component that may help with connecting is using items that tie to each of the Gods as offerings, or points of reverence.

For instance, Freyr could have a farm implement and be offered grain. Freyja could have a hawk feather, and be offered wine. Nerthus could have a bone, and be offered coins. Then Njord could be represented by shells, and be offered fish.

Invocation

Today we are here to honor the Vanir gods. Nerthus, Njord, Freyr, and Freyja. These are gods of nature, gods of shore and grain, gods of love, gods of war, gods of life and death. These gods are ancient, but we can feel them in our bones. We are all brothers and sisters of the Earth, carved from the same ash. We will be invoking each of these gods today, that they might hear your voices, that they might hear your call, and then, we will scream to them with a scream that will pierce the sky and take root in the earth!

Nerthus, life and death goddess, Queen of the Bog. She is the one who makes the berries you enjoy, and the berries that will kill you instantly. Hail to Nerthus!

Njord, we invoke you, Father of the Sea, Father of the Shining Twins - Freyr and Freyja. Though not every sea is calm, calm seas do not make for good sailors. Hail Njord!

Ingvi-Freyr, we welcome you here! One of the golden twins, a man's man who shows that masculinity is not pushing people down, but building them up, building yourself up so that you can build them as well. Growing together, loving together, Hail Freyr!

Freyja! Lady of the Vanir, Vanadis. We come to you today for blessings of love. Intoxicate us with your glory, drown us in beauty and lift us up stronger than we were before! Forge our bonds in your love. Hail Freyja!

All ritual participants come forward, one by one, and give their offerings, speaking words if they wish, and proclaiming to whom they are giving. After each offering, all folk hail the god or goddess who was offered to.

The plan for concluding the ritual was a final primal yell to the Vanir, but in practice, the ritual was concluded by the folk all jumping into a freezing lake together! It was an excellent impromptu moment of primality. Sometimes, chaotic improvisation leads to the best results.

Final Thoughts

Honoring a group of deities that share a common bond, such as the four major Vanir deities, is a great way to plan a larger and more complex ritual. Another aspect of this ritual that added to its power was the altar built for this occasion. Building an altar, mostly from items found in the wilderness, is an excellent way to honor the Gods, to enter the ritual mindset for those leading the ritual, and to provide an energetic focal point for everyone participating. This ritual can easily be adapted for the solo practitioner - find a powerful spot in nature, build an altar to the Vanir, and offer to each in turn. Jumping into a freezing lake is optional, but highly recommended!

Loki and Sigyn Ritual

By Lauren Gamble

The veneration of Loki and his family is often a debated topic in heathen spaces. We are lucky in our community to have folk who walk many different paths, and it's not uncommon to find a "Lokean", or three, amongst any gathering or event. Despite this, it seemed his rituals always tended toward small groups going off to give offerings in the woods. There is certainly a distinctly Loki vibe to adventuring off in the darkening forest to bare our souls to both one another and the God himself in relative privacy. But I felt it was time to bring our mischief maker into the light, as it were, to give him the same ritual pageantry that other Gods are afforded by our main nightly blóts.

Loki had been a part of my life for some time by the point I planned this ritual. A newer addition, however, was his wife Sigyn. I first reached out to her at Ohio Yule in December 2021. Loki's other children, and Angrboda herself, I had offered to previously but never felt a strong connection outside the obvious ancestral ties with Hel. Sigyn, I felt an immediate pull to after my first offering and promised I would do more research. So, I did. But there is, unfortunately, very little information on Sigyn outside of her marriage to Loki and the famous story of his snake-venom punishment.

It is this story which is the basis for the ritual of holding the bowl. By taking action and raising a bowl high you are offering your physical service and strength to Sigyn, allowing her to rest and be with her beloved so that they

Offering to Sigyn, Kentucky 2021

may receive their offerings together.

Invocation

I do not remember the exact words I spoke at this ritual and I never will, as I spoke directly from my heart and no video recording exists. But I will never forget the emotion those words held, and the gratitude that flowed through me as I finished my offering. I will outline an invocation below, but I urge you to fill in the gaps with your own personal stories of what Loki and Sigyn mean to you. Especially in a group setting, folk sharing stories and offerings while the ritual leader still holds the bowl allows an extended sacrifice and can help deepen a connection with the Goddess. Speaking from the heart authenticity is something both Loki and Sigyn value highly.

"Sigyn, Lady of Constancy,

Singer of Sorrow,

Mother of Narfi and Vali,

Innocent and Pure,

Wife of Loki,

Fire-bringer, Mischief Maker

I call to you Sigyn, Lady of Staying Heart

Let me hold the bowl this night,

Let our offerings bring you peace and strength,

Enjoy this time with your family

With Loki, bringer of laughter and joy

He who chases the truth

And is unafraid of the darkness that follows.

We honor you tonight, Loki and Sigyn

We honor your children, Narfi and Vali

We honor your extended family, who you hold so dear

Hel, Sleipnir, Fenrir, Jormungandr, Angrboda

We honor the loyalty and the love amongst chaos

Hail Loki!

Hail Sigyn!

Hail!"

When all offerings are given to the fire you may empty the bowl, and the ritual is completed. Say a few words about what the ritual meant to you and conclude the ceremony. I recommend a high content alcohol for the offering, as it symbolizes the venom quite well. Good non-alcoholic options would be vinegar or lemon juice, anything acidic.

Final Thoughts

Holding the Bowl as a ritual concept is well-known as a way to honor Sigyn, and quite frankly is one of the only unique rituals to her I have read. But rightfully so, as it is a very simple ritual to convert to a solo practice. Simply place a bowl on her altar, light a candle and/or some incense and lift the bowl into your arms. Recite the invocation or speak to Sigyn yourself, all while holding the bowl. When you are done, you may leave the offering within the bowl on your altar. You can do this practice as a form of meditation as well, or as a shorter everyday ritual practice.

I recommend speaking to Sigyn along with her family. She can get upset when her sons or husband are ignored, so it is common to begin work with her after being introduced via Loki. Her heart is compassionate and warm, but the depths of her pain and sorrow over the loss of her children is immense. She is gentle grace, she is fiery vengeance, and she is the master of her own destiny. Choice is everything, and Sigyn will remind you that choosing to be loyal and choosing love is the greatest blessing that you have. Loki will pester you until you finally end up laughing. I'm assuming you know what you're getting yourself into with him, if you've read this far on a Lokean ritual. But nevertheless. Don't take life too seriously, stick to what you believe in but keep an open mind, love fiercely and often, and take a good hard look in the mirror every morning. Stay wyrd, chaos crew!

Snotra Blót, Ohio 2022

Snotra Blót

By Kevin Roberts

The first time I gave Snotra an offering was at an open blót during the Autumn Gathering in Idaho in 2021. I had never worked with her at all, I just had some leftover honey and in the moment felt called to honor her. At that moment, I decided I needed to research her more and figure out why I felt the urge to give her an offering. The next day, as we were all loading vehicles and saying our goodbyes, I noticed all the different states' license plates. It was just a passing thought, that I would think back on later.

After getting home and looking more into Snotra, the aspect of tolerance and coming together kept focusing my attention. Then, the thought of all the different license plates, people from all over coming together at Gatherings and getting along hit me in a moment of clarity. At that point, I knew it was only right to honor and thank Snotra for her guidance during Gatherings.

Ritual

My ritual for Snotra is actually in two parts. The first on the first night of a Gathering, and the second on the final morning before leaving.

Friday night, spend a moment alone, speaking to Snotra, inviting her to join you, as you light candles and incense in a small circle in front of you. Once you are ready, invite the others to join you.

81

"Hail Snotra!
Goddess of wisdom.
Goddess of prudence.
Goddess of tolerance.
Goddess of social grace and courtesy."

In days gone by, our Ancestors gathered in halls. For celebration and for survival. Different families, villages, and nations came together, and sometimes tempers ran hot. In these times, the wise turned to Snotra to keep the peace. Violence sometimes occurred, of course, but Snotra's calming presence kept it from getting out of hand.

In our modern world, at Gatherings like this, it is only smart for us to ask for Snotra's guidance as well. We come from different towns, states, and even countries. We live different lives, have different priorities, different politics, different personalities. It is important to remember that here, none of that matters. We are here to celebrate that which unites us. Personality differences are inevitable, but with Snotra's guidance, we can ignore trivial differences and show true tolerance for those around us.

At this time, place your rock in the center of the candle circle, and invite all others to do the same, while saying aloud what state, province, county, or country you are from. After everyone has placed their rock, take a drink of mead, then pass it around for the others to join you. Then, pour the heavy cream onto the rock cairn.

This cairn symbolizes our coming together. Different rocks, and people, from all over, coming together to celebrate. As we all take a drink, let us remember that we are all in this together. Focus on that which unites us. Let this cairn stand as a reminder of that this weekend. Just like this cream [pour the cream over the cairn] let us thank and honor Snotra for her cool demeanor, sweet words, and calming presence.

Hail Snotra!

Monday morning (or, the last day of the Gathering), before everyone leaves, meet again at the cairn. Reflect for a minute on how the Gathering went. Say again how we are a group of different people, all coming together. Remember this feeling of peace, tolerance, and acceptance as we go back to our daily lives. At this time, each person takes a rock, NOT the one they brought, from the cairn. These rocks will serve as reminders of this feeling, kept on their altars, by their front door, in the garden, anywhere they want. Hopefully they will bring a bit of peace and calming presence into their homes.

Final Notes

After the first time I held this ritual, I felt the call to continue it at every Gathering I went to in the next year. I didn't want it to be exactly the same, so each time I changed it slightly. The beauty of this ritual that I've found, is that it is very easy to make small tweaks yet keep the essence. Lemon balm, chamomile, ginger, turmeric, mint, and rosemary can all be used instead of, or in addition to, the lavender. Having everyone hold a stick of incense can be very powerful. At one international Gathering, we used coins from everyone's home country instead of rocks.

I am so happy for that initial urge to offer to Snotra! This ritual has now become common at Gatherings, and I love that she is getting more attention and honor. Coming from a guy that has a close relationship with Tyr my whole life, her calming presence and guidance of tolerance is much needed!

When adapting this ritual for personal practices I recommend collection stones whenever you travel to friends or family, even if it's to a nearby family member. Through these small moments of fellowship and family you can build a small cairn on your altar, or in your garden to reflect on what Snotra teaches us. We don't always get along with friends and family; Snotra can be the glue that binds us together during those hard times, and these small stones allow us the time to reflect on that.

Thor Toast and Boast

By Keenan Long

This is actually a very commonly known ritual that I took and put my own spin on. The normal ritual goes as follows:

You gather in a location and the ritual leader will invoke the god, goddess, spirit, or entity you wish to toast or boast to. This can also just be done to give praise to those of your community as a sort of commemoration style ritual by building each other up. A leader will start the ritual by toasting to whomever they wish to direct it towards, or boasting to those gathered on themselves or another that is present. They will then pass attention on to another. In our case we used a hand-made cedar Mjolnir that we passed around as each person made their toast or boast. This can also be done with a large mead horn or any other item you see fit. This will repeat as many times as needed until all in attendance have made their toast or boast. Which at this time will be passed back to the ritual leader who will close out the ritual.

In traditional heathen circles this ritual is similar to a "Sumble/Symble" and is one of the main elements of religious veneration in many heathen groups. The details may change between groups, but it is common for the toasts and boasts to go for three rounds before it concludes.

Keenan holding his Mjolnir, North Carolina 2022

Invoking the Thunderer

Now that you understand the ritual, I'd like to walk you through how I opened this particular ritual invoking Thor and how I closed it out at the end.

We gathered in a small dining hall each with our mead in hand. I stood before them with the ritual Mjolnir and spoke loudly saying:

"Thor, thunderer, breaker, shaker, riding through the skies! Hear me oh strongest of the Aesir! We have gathered here to toast and boast to your greatness! Come and sit and revel with us as we drink and enjoy your company!"

At this point I transition from invoking to also boasting on the great feats of Thor.

"Thor the wielder of the mighty Mjolnir!
The one who fished the mighty Midgard serpent from the depths and lived to tell about it! The god who strikes fear in the hearts of every jotunn! The one who drank from the cup of Utgardr and drained the seas! The one who fought old age and was only taken to a knee! The one who at Ragnarok will slay the mighty Jormungandr at the last battle! Hail to Thor! The Protector of Midgard! Hail!

I then raised the hammer into the air as we hailed Thor together. This is where I then handed the hammer off to the next individual and the toast and boast began.

Now as we neared the end of our reveling. The last person finished and handed the hammer back to me once more. I stood before the room raising the hammer to the sky saying. "Hail to Thor and Hail to the Folk gathered here today! May the Thunder god bless each and everyone of you. For I know he is here with us right now. Thank you Thor for joining us today and enjoying the festivities. May you continue to protect us forever and always! Hail Thor! And Hail the Folk!!"

Final Thoughts

This ritual is better in a group environment, and is a great ice breaker for new faces at an event, as it gets us out of our shell. But this ritual can be adapted for the solo-practitioner who can sit before their sacred space and offer up their accomplishments to Thor. While this may feel awkward at first because we are not used to boasting about ourselves; Thor is a god of boasting, accomplishments, and overcoming challenges, so to share in these moments with him can be a great way to embody and honor Thor.

Goddess Blót

By Mary Grace and Logan Osborne

This ritual was one of our most complicated to plan and execute. This ritual is best with two people if possible, otherwise can be performed by one person; just prepare for a longer ritual! This was originally planned as one of the "main" rituals for a Yule event and took well over 45 minutes to perform. However it was certainly worth the time and devotion; many people were in tears by the end and it proved to be very powerful.

Within Norse Mythology there are many goddesses; in fact, if the handmaidens of Frigg are counted there are more listed Goddesses than there are Aesir and Vanir Gods. And yet despite this, we have very little information about them. That is the aim of this ritual, to name these beings and their known attributes with personalized offerings based on these attributes. While it can be hard to create 20+ unique offerings, it is worth the effort if planned in advance. However, similar offerings presented to each of the Goddesses are also perfectly acceptable.

Invocation

First we give to the **Disir**, the women of millennia past, without whom no one would live. May they accept this gift and continue to watch over us and impart wisdom, love, and good fortune.

Next we give to **Frigg** and her handmaidens, the high queen of Asgard. She who sits upon the throne and sees and knows only what she can know. May we, like her, be wisdom inspired in deep knowing. Hail to you, great mother.

Freyja, Vanadis, lady of the vanir. Goddess of love and war. Goddess of magic and beauty. She who taught Odin. Queen of Folkvangr, guide us as you guided him. Hail Freyja.

Idunn, goddess of the fruits which keep the gods immortal. Your actions granting life everlasting. May we create the kind of life for ourselves that we would wish to go on forever. Hail Idunn.

To **Mengloth**, seldom remembered, the necklace glad healer of herself. May we be steadfast in our own healing. May we be like her. Hail Mengloth.

To **Skadi**, snow-queen, ice-goddess of the winter. Goddess of the hunt and of sport. May we come to know you during this time. Hail Skadi.

Sif, your gifts have fed our ancestors for time immemorial. May we remember you in this time of bounty. Thank you for providing for us. Hail Sif.

Sigyn, she who bears the bowl of venom beneath the Earth. Your story is an example of love and eternal loyalty. May we all seek to embody your loyalty. May your arms never tire and may our hearts never empty. Hail Sigyn.

Goddess Blót, Ohio 2021

To **Hel**, goddess of the dead and of the underworld. Goddess who greets our ancestors in her embrace. May we too find comfort when we find ourselves at your gates. Hail Hel.

Gullveig, the gold-thirsty, thrice-burned and thrice-returned. Your death led to the Aesir-Vanir war that united the gods. You arose from the ashes as the luster of gold, may we do the same in our own trials. Hail Gullveig.

To **Ran**, the ocean is in a sense the mother of us all - the origin of all life. A deep well of mystery and power. May we gaze into those bottomless waters and gain wisdom from what we find there. Hail Ran.

To **Hnoss and Gersemi**, the daughters of Freyja, treasure and jewel. May we all find beauty and abundance in the world and in ourselves. Hail Hnoss and Gersemi.

Nerthus, matron of the Vanir. Mother of the golden twins. The bog queen. Goddess of the cycle of life and death, eternal. Hail Nerthus.

To **Nott**, dream met goddess of wisdom. Goddess who forces us inside for this time of night. May we remember you, may we honor you, grandmother of Thor. Hail Nott.

To **Angrboda**, the wolf queen, mistress of the iron-wood. May we all respect such a force of unbridled power. Hail Angrboda.

Jord, Goddess of the Earth. Nothing that we know is not you. We are your children along with the plants and animals. What can we give you that is not yours? Hail Jord.

Eir, I offer to you in hopes that you will continue to help us heal. I know many of us who are sick in our hearts, minds, or bodies. I offer to you for them. Hail Eir.

Gerdr, rebellious-one admired by Freyr, goddess of the areas untouched by man or machine. May we remember to connect to our innate wildness in this time of concrete and steel. Hail Gerdr.

To the wife of Baldur, **Nanna**, goddess of peace. I offer up a creation from my grief. May you bring peace to those in need. Hail Nanna.

Saga, inspiration-goddess who writes the tales Odin tells. She who drinks from his same cups. May we too swim in those waters. Hail Saga.

To **Sunna**, shining source of heat, light, and life. Your rebirth is upon us as the wheel spins. We rejoice in your rays. Hail Sunna.

To the **Norns**: Urdr, Verthandi, and Skuld. The past, old Urdr; the present, the ever changing Verthandi; Skuld, the young future not yet told. May our carvings on the roots of Yggdrasil reign true and may they be. Hail to the Norns.

We have offered to many goddesses tonight, all deserving of our praise. It's a sad truth that many goddesses have been forgotten. There are goddesses that we only know for single word associations, but there are still those among us who seek to rekindle their flame. We also give to the forgotten goddesses, may we remember them.

"The wheel has spun around
...through the seasons and back to here

The feminine guides intuition
...may we learn our lessons well

Many blessings upon all who honor the goddesses
...through their actions and devotion

Goddesses, our thanks and praise go to you!
Our cycles begin anew."

Final Thoughts

We believe in the worship of our Goddesses. They are often forgotten in favor of masculine deity worship, but they are also powerful and guiding forces that have a great impact upon their devotees. Even without offerings, taking the time to acknowledge the many different known goddesses in a single ritual is a powerful experience in itself.

Calling the Spirits, Minnesota 2022

The Spirits

By Aayla Kaisk and Claire Beukinga

The belief in spirits is integral to any pagan path, as animism is the basis of these traditions. Animism is the belief that spirits are connected to the world around us, and that we can interact with them. These spirits are different from working with deities like Odin or Frigg, because they are more in touch with the everyday actions and are tied intimately with the evolution of our lives, whereas the gods and goddesses are entities we can entreat and devote ourselves to, but they rarely interfere with humans. This can be shown when you read the sagas.

When we talk about giving offerings or communicating with these spirits, it is with the knowledge that they are as alive as we are. There are many different types of spirits. Some of the more well known and worked with are:

Landvættir - Various land spirits
Alfar - Elf spirits
Disir - Female ancestors
Hausvættir - House spirits
Nisse or Tomte - A type of hausvættr
Wights - Spirits associated with objects

It is up to you and your journey to discover your own connection to these spirits, to forge a relationship that will bring you and the spirits goodwill and blessings.

You may also be surprised at the ones who reach out to you throughout your journey.

There are many different ways in which to make offerings to the different spirits you will come across as your practice evolves. Landvættir love biodegradable foods, things that would be found naturally in the area that you are giving the offering. Look into what is native in your region, what foods grow naturally where you are, what herbs and flowers grow there. This will guide you in making powerful offerings to the local spirits. You can build simple outdoor altars, or make the offerings in natural hollows of trees, or by rivers.

"Let me feel the earth breath beneath my feet, as I sync myself with your breathing heart.
Let my skin emerge with the soil and let my blood flow within me like fresh water.
Let my arm stretch like the branches of your oldest trees and let my breath be fleeting like a soft wind breeze.
Let the sun charge my soul and let the moon acknowledge my emotions, for all may be.

For that I am grateful"

Be careful of the rivers and waterways, these have been decimated in modern times and spirits can be angry if the offering isn't in the best interest of the water health wise. Always do your research. Offerings will vary based on which spirits you are working with, and the season that you are working in. You can also get as specific as looking at the astrological time as well if that is something you are interested in and part of your practice.

At home you can build a small altar indoors, typically in the heart of the home like the kitchen, to give offerings and build a solid relationship with the spirit of your home. Your hausvættr is your first defense, so give it offerings when you cook, or if you bring home a tasty treat. Keep the area clean, organized, and show through your actions that you have love and gratitude for your home.

The kitchen is also a great place for your ancestor altar, both for the disir and male ancestors. This keeps them present in your mind every day, and in my experience makes them feel included to see the comings and goings of their family so they can watch over you and offer advice easier, as it is like they aren't really gone.

Kitchens were, and still very much are, the heart of the family home. It is where we gather every day, multiple times a day, and our energy individually and as a family unit, whatever form that takes for you, builds in this part of the home. Therefore it makes a powerful place for hausvættir and ancestor altars. Be creative and let the altars you build be a reflection of you, your family, and your special connection to these spirits. Outdoors, altars can be as simple or as elaborate as you want, keeping in mind your purpose and connection. Some people like to place them in a specific Cardinal direction in the yard, or travel to a special location in a public park. Whatever or wherever you build your space is up to you. Intention is the root of everything.

A word of caution. Balance is the basis of all paths and traditions, we see this acutely in nature. This is no different when working with spirits. There are good spirits, helpful spirits, joyful spirits, silly spirits; but we also have malevolent spirits, trickster spirits, trouble makers, and negative or depressive spirits. They are as essential to life and ritual as the positive ones. For example, if you are a person prone to depression and come across a spirit that feeds this in you and you continually try to 'banish' it, maybe sit with this spirit. Ask it what it wants, give it an offering of alcohol (a traditional offering for underworld spirits or ancestors). Over time a reciprocal relationship can form and this entity or spirit can then feed off your depression, taking it as an offering and alleviating yourself of this spirit from embodying you. Protection is always key, and very important during any ritual, big or small.

The concept of spirits is a complicated one, but don't let this complexity scare you away from what can be some of the most genuine and wholesome connections you will find in spiritual practices!

Ritual to the Landvættir
By Mary Grace

Land honoring rituals generally happen on the first day of our events. These are designed to give thanks to the spirits for being our hosts and also to let them know we seek their friendship. The first day of a gathering can be a little tense with both new and old faces arriving throughout the day and getting settled. Singing and dancing together is an excellent way to loosen up for the weekend ahead. And so these acts are combined through a song called *"Komme Komme Alle."*

"Komme Komme Alle" is an original Norwegian song written by Volva Kari Tauring. The song is simple to memorize and chant and contains some runes as well, creating a sort of galdr-song. The song translates to:

"Come, come all, all sing Ehol (Algiz), Gifu (Gebo) Gifu (Gebo) Man-home, come come all."

To paraphrase, the song essentially means:

"Come here to us, all sing together of protection and divine intention, we have gifts for you, come come all!"

A fitting song to dance among offerings and new friends while honoring the land spirits.

"Komme Komme Alle
Alle Singen Ehol
Gifu Gifu Mannaheim
Komme Komme Alle"

It is recommended to repeat this several times, until you feel the energy build to a point of connection. This song is great to sing alone in nature! So don't be afraid to sing to the spirits, it's something all of our ancient ancestors did to feel connected.

Ritual the the Lanvættir, North Carolina 2022

Ancestor Ritual

By Jacob Toddson

The idea for this ritual came to me when preparing for our first English Gathering in the community. For me personally, to travel to a place I know my ancestors are from was a very exciting thought. So I really wanted to develop a ritual that would connect me with those ancestors in a very deep way. That is where I came up with the mud.

The mud for me, was a symbol of where we all end up when we die, we all return to the earth. We all become nothing eventually. So to rub the mud onto our own bodies in this way, is showing that we accept that one day we all become a part of the mud.
Now the spiritual side of the mud, is that depending how much you cover yourself with, this would determine how deep the ritual would get for you. So to cover just your hands, or your face would be a light experience. But when you start rubbing the mud into your torso, and legs. You are really looking for a deep experience.

Especially since this is a long commitment, as the mud takes a long time to harvest, apply, and then remove. Really plan for several hours to perform this ritual by yourself. And it is best to have others with you that you trust, as you will be very vulnerable both spiritually and literally, as you are in theory outside somewhere covered in mud.

Now having said that I do think a smaller version of this ritual can easily be performed within your own home, just reduce the amount of mud you use, perhaps you are painting runes with the mud, or just covering a small amount of your body. Regardless, I think this ritual is very adaptable to anyone's needs.

Final notes on the mud: it should be harvested as locally as possible to where you live. However if you are traveling and collect dirt from somewhere and are able to bring it back, this will also create a very powerful effect if you so choose.

While this ritual is pretty out there, there are some historical and mythological inspirations behind it. The main mythological influence for this ritual was the stories of Odin, and Freyja, calling out to the dead, and bringing them back to life. Oftentimes they did this to seek prophecy and understanding of the future.

In a personal environment you will enact less as this undead beacon, but more as someone wishing to connect more with their ancestors. Even with that, this ritual is very heavy, and does require a certain amount of spiritual protection in order to ensure that it works properly and safely.

Safety and protection

Anytime you are working with beings from the lower world or afterlife, it is important to have as many things possible to protect you on your journey. I highly recommend cleansing whatever space you use for this

103

Ancestor Mud Ritual, England 2022

with whatever smudging implement you prefer. Personally for me I invoke gods of protection, as well as spirits, to ensure a safe ritual. I have several Fylgia (Norse animal spirits) that I use during these rituals, as well as protective charms which I wear around my neck that represent the gods, ancestors, and spirits that I call to. What you use for your ritual will most likely be different, and personal to you. The most important part is that you use spiritual protection.

As far as sacred places, you can perform this at your altar space, using a light amount of mud as I described earlier. However if you wish to perform this ritual in the wild then I recommend building a sacred circle out of stones and sticks - possibly even adding runes such as Algiz for protection.

If you are outside, I highly recommend clearing the space fully clothed before you dress down to what you feel comfortable wearing. During my first performance of this ritual, I found old nails by the fire after I performed it, and luckily, I did not step on them. So please be safe physically when doing this.

And once again, I highly recommend that if you perform this out in the wild, have someone there with you. That way they can stop anyone from interrupting you, answer any questions that may come up, and just be there for you through an intense ritual.

Offerings

Anytime you perform a ritual I recommend having gifts for whoever you are contacting, and during heavier rituals, I always give offerings to the spirits of the land, gods, and ancestors to ensure a successful ritual. These offerings can be small, I have even given from the same bottle of liquor to each of the beings I call to. But I will say the more layers you add to each step of a ritual will only help you in the effects of whatever ritual you are performing.

Good offerings for this ritual : fruits, vegetables, breads, wine, ciders and juices, made objects such as: notes, idols, or trinkets.

Fire is always the best way in my opinion to give offerings to the gods, but in the case of this ritual the original plan was to bury the offerings for the ancestors. And if you are at your own altar space, giving small offerings to a single offering bowl that you can take out into nature after the ritual is what I recommend.

Performance

After setting up the space, whether that is in the wild or at your home altar, call to the deities in any way you feel comfortable. I recommend honoring the gods, ancestors, and the spirits in every ritual before focusing on the subject of the ceremony.

"To the spirits of the land, I call to you in order to carry my words far.
To the ancestors below I beckon you to hear my words, and give me guidance.
To the Aesir, I call for your wisdom, your protection, and your blessings for this ritual."

I typically leave a small offering, even just a small amount of a liquid, to each of these beings for their attention. I will then draw attention to the main focus of the ritual, the mud.

"In this bowl, I have mud of the earth. May it symbolize that in the end we all must return to our earth mother. To Jord, the mother of Thor, and the lover of the Allfather Odin. Our bones will turn to dust, or flesh to dirt, and our name only remaining in memory. This mud symbolizes all the ancestors who came before me, and all those who will come after me. As I place it on my skin, may it connect me to the lines of ancestors all around me."

Then place the mud on your body to whatever extent you feel comfortable, I recommend starting with the hands, and then working your way up from there. Keep in mind that mud can often be hard to get out of certain places!

Once the mud has been applied, you may give offerings to the ancestors in general, or to specific ancestors that you wish to connect with. Spend as much time with this step as you would like.

After you feel comfortable and satisfied it is time to close the ritual by thanking the forces that have joined you. Allow the ancestors to return to the spirit world, and send them with love in your heart. Then close the space similar to how you opened it:

"To the spirits of the land, I thank you for carrying my voice across midgard.
To the ancestors below, I thank you for hearing my words and giving me guidance.
And to the Aesir, I thank you for your wisdom, protection, and your blessings for this ritual."

Now it is time to clean the mud off of your body. I recommend a water hose if you are outside, a dip in a stream, or washing off with a bucket of water. If you are in your house, then wash your hands or take a shower if necessary. This ritual will be as clean or messy as you'd feel like, so just keep that in mind when deciding how much mud you use, and where you perform it.

Final Thoughts

When I first performed this ritual in the UK I was really taken back by how powerful it was for everyone there. It seemed to really help everyone connect to the earth and to the departed. The mud was a really powerful element, as it marked ourselves in a very primal way for the time that we were covered in it. And yes, it was incredibly hard to get off, and was quite cold with the water hose we had access to. I hope this ritual helps you connect with your ancestors!

RITES OF PASSAGE

Marriage Ceremony

By Jacob Toddson

Marriage has been around since at least 2400 BCE, and more than likely has existed before then. This is because the concept of love transcends cultures, and has been at the very core of humanity in our known histories. This is no different in the ancient north, where the tradition of hand-fasting has been a part of folk ceremonies for hundreds of years. Like many rituals and traditions of the ancient world, we do not know specifics of how the people from the old north tied the knot, we only know that they did. The Romans would observe the marriage customs of the Germanic and Celtic people. We also have some record of the laws around marriage from medieval Iceland.

There are several deities to consider when looking at marriage, such as: Thor, Freyjr and Bragi. Then for goddesses there are: Freyja, Frigg, Sif, Idunn, and more notably the handmaidens of Frigg. Sjofn and Lofn are two of Frigg's handmaidens that are stated in the *Prose Edda* to create love in the hearts of men and women, and to bring men and women together in marriage, despite the challenges around it. Var is another handmaiden that oversees oaths, and seeks punishment for the oath breakers; however divorce– if done properly between both parties–can be handled in a way that nullifies the oath of love, rather than break it.

Notes on preparation

This ceremony is highly customizable to those getting married, and whomever is preparing the ceremony. Various deities, ritual items, and offerings can be added, or not added, depending on personal preferences. For the sake of this section, a ceremony using hand-fasting will be described as it was performed at a marriage at a Midsummer event in Kentucky. Using wedding rings, oath rings, and other items to swear oaths on are perfectly acceptable. What is most important is the oath swearing itself.

Final note: The Fellowship of Northern Traditions and its clergy, Fellowship Leaders, are able to perform legal weddings within the United States. If you wish to have one of our leaders perform a wedding ceremony for you, please email us at fellowshipofnortherntraditions@gmail.com. We believe love is love, and are happy to perform weddings for any couple.

Performance

Call out to the cardinal directions, asking them to witness a celebration of love. If you have offerings to share this will be the time to give them. In the past a horn of mead has been poured out between each cardinal direction. For example:

Marriage Ceremony, Kentucky 2022

"I call to the North, the sacred direction from which the Gods originated. I call to you Sjofn, to you Lofn, and to you Var to witness this celebration of love." *Pour out some mead*

"I call to the East, to the realm of the rising sun…" *Pour out some mead*

"I call to the South, the direction of our seasonal changes…" *Pour out some mead*

"I call to the West, the realm of the setting sun…" *Pour out some mead*

In each direction you can insert whatever deity you wish to call to and add in whatever verse you would like to use to call to them. It is also recommended that you call to the spirits of the lands to bless the marriage, as well as the ancestors of both families to join in celebration. For instance the eastern "hail" can be to the families of spouse #1, and the western "hail" can be to the ancestors of spouse #2. Then the southern "hail" can be to the spirits of the land. Ultimately it is your choice, the main focus is to introduce what is happening to the spiritual presences around us.

At this point have the couple join hands and wrap whatever cloth you are using around both hands and arms. Make sure the couple are facing one another and are comfortable. No need to make the tying too tight, only secure. Announce to the audience, and to each spouse why you are binding their hands, and what it symbolizes.

Once the knot has been tied, allow each spouse a moment to recite their oaths to one another.

Now the couple kiss!

To close the ceremony essentially do everything in reverse. Untie the couple's hands, and announce to the world and the gods that they are now married! Lot's of cheering and celebrating should follow. Be sure to thank the spiritual presences that you have called to, preferably in the reverse order that you called to them in. Once gratitude has been given the party is allowed to commence; now, celebrate love!

One tradition that has been recorded in the folk traditions of northern Europe is having a "race" back to the house, or the location of the reception. This should be done between the two joining families, whoever gets back first gets bragging rights (and gets to eat first). Marriages should be a fun, memorable celebration of love and life. So get creative with it, and remember the more you celebrate the more the Gods will join you!

Final Thoughts

It can be really hard to write a marriage ceremony, because it will change based on so many factors. Just remember the elements to keep sacred are: the calling out to the Gods, Spirits and Ancestors, the swearing of the oaths, and thanking the Gods, Spirits, and Ancestors. Everything after that should be fluid, fun, and allow room for creativity.

Baby Naming Ceremony

By Nils the Ironwolf

The baby naming ceremony traditionally took place 10 days after the child was born (to ensure the baby would survive after birth). When the baby was given a name, they were considered legitimate in their community and able to inherit lands and property. The ritual was known as "Vatni Ausa" meaning to pour or sprinkle water over. The ceremonies were undertaken for both girls and boys:

"Then in the summer when Þórsteinn was twenty-five years old, Þóra gave birth to another son, who was sprinkled with water and given the name Grímr. Þórsteinn dedicated this boy to Þórr, calling him Þórgrímr."
(Eyrbyggja saga, chapter 11)

"In the summer Þóra gave birth to a girl, who was sprinkled with water and given the name Ásgerðr."
(Egils saga Skallagrímssonar, chapter 35)

The ceremony would begin with the baby being picked up, usually by the father, from the ground. This is thought to be an act of acceptance. The naming rite was seen as the official moment the baby became part of the family and when they became protected under law.

Water would then be sprinkled on the child. This practice pre-dates the Christianization of the region and is subtly yet distinctly different from baptism. In baptism the water is to "purify" the child, referred to in old Norse during the later Christian period as "skirn" meaning purification. In the pre-Christian Vatni Ausa ceremony the water was to "hallow" meaning to bless or make sacred, essentially, a blessing from the Gods.

The "hallowing" or blessing was completed with the sign of the hammer being made over the child, referencing or invoking the protection of the God Thor. Thor, despite his mighty hammer wielding image, is also the protector and blesser of all humankind.

Final Thoughts

As with the marriage ceremony there is plenty of room for creativity and personal choices within this ritual. It can be a big, or small affair. In our modern era children are given very little spiritual ritual outside of the church. Remember, this is a ceremony of celebration!

After a Baby Naming Ceremony, Ohio 2022

Funeral

By Jacob Toddson

It can be hard to look at funerals as celebrations during our times of grief, however from what we know of the ancient past, they were times of celebration. Death is very stigmatized in many parts of the world, mainly in parts where monotheistic world views are most prominent.

From what we know of the burial customs of the ancient peoples of Northern Europe, death is a journey. One you must be prepared for with food, drink, and possibly even weapons and home goods. Board games have also been a common grave good found across burial mounds in the ancient world! With the current monotheistic worldview dominating burial practices, it can be hard to meet the "pagan" image of death in our preferences on burial.

What we hope this section will provide is a starting point for that conversation. Please note that these might not all be possible within your region, and they would more than likely require approval from your city or other local authority that controls burial laws.

Burial or Cremation?

Within history we find evidence of both burials and cremations across the northern world. From boat graves, to burial mounds, to simple monument stones; there is a wide range of options available to those looking to have a modern pagan funeral. However, adapting this to modern requirements can be tricky, so once again understand this section should help inspire, rather than be treated as law.

For burials we can no longer build burial mounds and have vast boats buried with us. But what is possible is being buried with some grave goods in your casket. While you cannot be buried with a massive horde like the ancient past, you could still choose several small items to be placed in your casket, such as:

- Small packages of food such as bread, grains, fruits, vegetables or smoked meats.
- Bottles of mead, juice, beer, or liquor.
- Small valuables such as coins, rings, necklaces, or gems.
- Entertainment such as books, or board games.
- Historic weapons like swords, daggers, axes, or a small shield.
- Spiritual objects of significance

The amount of objects will be up to local burial laws and limitations, but if there is one important lesson we learn from burial graves of the past it's that you bring items with you into the next life!

As far as cremation, this is where things get a little more complicated. The image of big funeral pyres with the dead being carried away to the afterlife, is a powerful one, butthis cremation style is not legal in most places.

What would need to be done is to have your body cremated through certified and regulated means, and request that your ashes be sent to family, friends, or your local pagan community. Preferably your ashes will be stored in a wooden box before the ceremony is able to be planned.

The ceremony itself will involve a funeral "pyre" where the ashes are placed in the center with any objects from the previous list. The benefit of this method is that it will allow you to be cremated with more personal belongings, and be done in a much more pagan, more spirituall way.

It is ultimately up to the individual how their remains are treated, and there is evidence for both burial and cremation in the ancient past. However, one section from *Ynglinga Saga* shows there was a preference for cremation in ancient Scandinavia.

"Thus Odin established by law that all dead men should be burned, and their belongings laid with them upon the pile, and the ashes be cast into the sea or buried in the earth. Thus, said he, every one will come to Valhalla with the riches he had with him upon the pile; and he would also enjoy whatever he himself had buried in the earth. For men of consequence a mound should be raised to their memory, and for all other warriors who had been distinguished for manhood a standing stone; which custom remained long after Odin's time."

-Ynglinga Saga, Snorri Sturluson

Now to cover what can be done and said during a ritual around a funeral when the fated day arrives:

Ritual

We are lucky enough at The Fellowship of Northern Traditions, that we have not performed a funeral yet for our community and its members. But we are not blind to the reality of life, and the acceptance that we will one day have to do so. For the sake of this section I will share a possible ritual for a funeral, from the perspective of a cremation:
Once the funereal pyre is prepared and all have gathered around, the ritual leader can come forward.

"We are gathered here today in a time of sadness, that we hope to turn into a night of celebration. I call to the Gods of Death to witness this celebration of life! To Odin, and your Valkyries! To Freyja in Folkvangr! To Hel in her hall of the dead! To Ran and Aegir in their depths below the sea!

To the ancestors we call so that they may receive another into their loving embrace. We send our beloved to you on the steed of fire, may it carry them, and their possessions to you in one piece!"

At this point the fire can be lit

As the fire begins to burn, friends and family can come forward and share stories and speak of the departed. The focus should be on the good stories of the departed, not the bad. Focus on what they should be

121

remembered for. For the times they made people laugh, or the good deeds they performed from their heart in life. Tears and sadness are natural to us when we lose our loved ones, but they would not want us to cry; they would want us to celebrate with them. That is how we keep their memory alive.

Once the fire begins to die down, the ritual leader can step in and close the ritual by thanking the Gods and Spirits, acknowledging the ancestors for their time, and allowing the departed to join them. This is also a chance for the ritual leader to continue raising everyone's spirits in celebration of life, and the natural passage of death.
In pagan beliefs death is not the end, it is simply another beginning.

"Who shall sing me,
Into deathsleep sling me,
Whence I on the path to Hel go,
And this track I tread
Is cold, so cold, so cold.
Once you stand at the gate to Hel
And when you have to tear free,
I shall follow you
Over Gjallarbru with my song.

You will be free from the bonds that bind you,
You are free from the bonds that bound you!"

-Lines from *Helvegen* by the band Wardruna

Oath Swearing Ceremony
By Heath Gore

What is an oath? While some will debate whether there is a difference between swearing an oath and making a simple promise, oaths are usually a lifelong commitment, or at the very least until the objective of the oath is fulfilled. Oaths should be taken with the utmost respect and seriousness. There are sources in the surviving texts that have come down to us that show that oaths were a very important and sacred thing to the ancient Norse cultures. It is also shown to us that the Gods do not look favorably on those who break their oaths.

In this modern day some choose to wear an "oath ring" which is a metal arm band that is worn on the wrist or upper arm. These arm bands have been in burial graves across Europe. However, their usage as' 'oath rings' ' is not known to us. Modern Asatru adherents will often use a much larger oath ring that will be held in the hand of a "priest" and then in the hand of the oath swearer.

There is also a story that comes to us from the Orkney Islands where a stone called "The Odin Stone" was used to swear oaths, make promises, and swear marriage vows. This stone featured a hole that two people would place their arms through and hold hands to make promises. These promises were considered law in the eyes of the community. So while we do not have specific evidence to say that personally worn 'oath rings' were ever used in the ancient past, the act and importance of swearing an oath was incredibly important.

With oaths being this sacred, the real question you should start asking yourself is "Is having a ceremony necessary?".

Ceremony

Create your sacred space either at an altar or in nature. Prepare whatever object you wish to swear your oath onto, this can be a ring, rock, necklace, sword - really whatever calls to you. Once you've done this, begin to invoke the Gods, the land spirits, and the ancestors. Invite them to come and bear witness to the oath that will be sworn. Give an offering if you feel it is needed, then place your hand on the object and swear your oath. Once you have completed this step, you may put on the item if possible, or place the object in a pocket or secure place. As always, close the ritual by thanking the Gods and Spirits for bearing witness before dismissing them.

It is important to remember that the loss of the ring or item does not remove the oath, and it is possible to replace a broken object with another - simply repeat the ritual for that new object.

This should be viewed as a solemn ceremony. You've said the words, now it's time for you to live by it. This cannot be stressed enough.

Final thoughts

Depending on your situation, you can change the structure of this ceremony in any way to fit your own needs. However, I do want to stress that oaths are not necessary, should be carefully thought out, and should always be followed up with action. I've hopefully made clear the importance of oath keeping; an individual should face that risk on their own terms. So I hope you'll keep that in mind if you do a ritual or ceremony such as this. I will add at the end here, that an oath can be a powerful tool if used well and maintained. Oaths can keep us honest and help improve our lives when handled properly.

GRATITUDE

The most powerful force in the spiritual world is gratitude. Gratitude to the Gods for their guidance, gratitude for the spirits for their beauty, gratitude for the ancestors and their sacrifices. This book was brought to life through the work of leadership within the Fellowship of Northern Traditions. A group of individuals that started off simply as some friends wanting to have fun and worship the Gods. What it has turned into is so much more than we could have ever dreamed of.

From all of the leadership, we are so grateful to walk this path with all of those who have attended our events and been a part of this community throughout the years. And to the individuals who have simply purchased this book for the sake of their own research, we hope it has been helpful and entertaining. We do not pretend for a second that we know all of the answers to the rituals of the ancient past, and how they should be practiced today. We simply have done our best to create unique rituals that honor that ancient past, while still allowing for imagination and evolution.

The Fellowship of Northern Traditions officially started in 2022, and as of the completion of this book we have raised over $18,000 to purchase our own plot of land to leave a legacy for the future generations. The proceeds of this book will also assist us in reaching our goal to purchase land, and build a place of permanence for our traditions to continue to grow through the generations.

We have a long road ahead of us, one we are so grateful to be on. Thank you from the bottom of our hearts for coming along with us, and being a part of this strange, and wonderful journey!

-The Fellowship

Community Website:
www.northerntraditions.org

The Fellowship Leaders, 2022 (Not pictured: Maya Hany, Terry Holtom, Claire Beukinga, Nicholas Camp, Caleb Baker)

Made in the USA
Coppell, TX
04 September 2023

21198512R00072